Fabulous Functions
for the
Faint-Hearted

A Simple Guide to Event Planning

GW00505792

DEBORAH GRANVILLE

ISBN-13: 978-0-9935311-0-1
ISBN-10: 0993531105

DEDICATION

For M, S and I, and for my parents.

CONTENTS

INTRODUCTION

Ooh, I do love parties! Well, let me qualify that. I love parties that have content – not the ones where people have to balance a plate of food in one hand and a glass in the other, trying to shout over the music or lack of good acoustic management, asking politely where you come from or what you do, whilst trying not to look over their shoulders or winking at your partner to get you away from this boring person who is probably equally bored and longing to get into their jammies and watch *Strictly*. I love a party where there is stuff to do, whether it's a quiz, dancing, singing – oh, how I love a karaoke – playing games like charades, or categories, or even Cluedo. Don't get me wrong, the food and drink have to be good and there must be music, even if it's in the background - a party isn't a party without sounds - and there should be, ideally, a good mix of people who really want to be there and celebrate the occasion.

So, this book is for you if you love a party or need to organise an event, but don't have the time and are daunted just thinking about what's involved – oh, the organisation, the hassle, the hoo-ha! Well, it is true that there can be hassle and hoo-ha, but if you follow my simple set of rules in the following chapters, I promise that it won't seem as daunting as you first thought. So choose your chapter and let's get started!

1 BIRTHDAYS, ANNIVERSARIES AND OTHER SIGNIFICANT DO'S

So, you want to organise a birthday/anniversary/thank you/congratulatory party. It could be yours, your child's, your husband's, your mother's, a friend's or even a work colleague's. Naturally, unless you are slightly perverse, you will want to hold the party on or as near as dammit to the date of the event to be celebrated, so choosing the date will be your first task. So if, for example, the birthday is on a Monday, it seems sensible to pick the Saturday following or preceding. What, I hear you cry? Have I bought this book so you can tell me the blindingly obvious? Well, no – because your preferred date is relevant to your budget – so if it suits you to have the event on a Thursday instead of at the weekend, it will be a lot cheaper. But do you really want to have a shindig on a school night? Follow me along the primrose path to party pleasure, with my 12 To Do's.

Decide on Budget

This is the absolutely vital first step when organising any event. Of course you will have thought about the party beforehand and imagined what you might like to have, but once you start the actual planning process you must, must,

must have a budget in mind that you can afford and try to stick to it. You do not want to be paying for this party for years afterwards and as a faint-heart the last thing you need is to be worrying about how you are going to earn enough to pay for what is, to be honest, a fleeting event in your life, however many wonderful memories it will create for you and your guests. Once you have decided on a budget, all other elements of the event will flow like, well, chocolate from a fountain!

Choose and Book Venue

There are thousands of venues in London alone, never mind in the rest of the UK. Every non- residential building now sees itself as a potential cash-raising cow, so your imagination is your only boundary. However, for faint-hearts it's usually best to stick to a tried and tested space.

Restaurants, pubs and bars will be your best bet. They either have a dedicated space for parties away from the main room or they will let you take over the whole or part of the venue. (You could choose a hotel, but in my experience they tend to be quite sterile environments, unless you have a huge budget and can afford to hire Grosvenor House). If the latter, there will probably be a minimum spend, which usually includes food and drink. If you don't want to use their in-house caterers, you can find what is called in the trade a 'dry hire' space. In London these are often spaces under the arches and are usually blank canvases for you to decorate as you desire. They can be a bit daunting for faint-hearts because not only will you have to find and bring in caterers, but also manage the space – there will be lots of to-ing and fro-ing between you, the caterers and the venue to ensure that everything the caterer needs is on site, or you'll end up incurring more costs if the caterers have to bring their own cooking facilities etc. Daunted already, eh? Of course, you could hold the party in your own house or garden with a marquee. There certainly are advantages to this in that you don't have to manage the issues surrounding hiring an external venue, but as a faint- heart, do you really want hordes of guests tramping through your house and garden, muddying your beautiful carpets, knocking over Great Aunty Margaret's priceless wedding gift and...oh, you do? Well, you get the picture. From a faint-heart's point of view, a party in one's own house is not a great idea, so if you can afford not to, and to be honest there probably won't be that much of a difference in price were you to consider hiring a marquee say, I would opt for an external venue.

Something else to consider when choosing a venue is accessibility. For example, is it close to public transport? Does it have a car park or are there parking facilities nearby? Does it have disabled access should that be needed? Make a little list of what's important to you about the venue before you start your search. And although I've placed this above choosing a theme, read on in case you decide to have a theme, because that may inform your venue choice.

Choose Theme

Choosing a theme can be fun! After all, if you're having a significant birthday, you might fancy a 60s or 90s night, or a James Bond night, or a Venetian Masked Ball (nice!) – and a theme can then inform your catering and music choices too. So here are a few ideas to get you in the mood:

Child's birthday: animals, TV or film characters are perennially popular.

Teenagers: music, TV and film will most likely dictate what a teenager would enjoy. Sweet 16 parties are currently very popular, but each teenage year will have something upon which to hang a theme. So 13 – first teenage year, 14 – start of GCSE year, 15 – last GCSE year, 17 – driving year, 18 – adulthood etc. Or you could use the year of their birth – probably more interesting for the parents!

Adults: year of birth is definitely good for adults, as are Hollywood, Bollywood, Boogie Nights, decades (20s/30s/40s/etc....), James Bond, Arabian Nights, Heaven and Hell.

And people like dressing up – well, I know men tend to say they don't, although I don't want to gender stereotype, in fact I think it can be more of an age thing, but I love it, so if you love it too, go for it and choose a theme where guests can dress up without it being too onerous a task, if you think there could be a bit of resistance – James Bond, or even Mods & Rockers or 80s/90s shouldn't be too much of a stretch for most. Or you could go for a colour: black and white, red, gold and silver.

Whatever you choose, someone will have a moan, but don't listen to them - go with your gut!

Invite Guests

Nowadays you can spend absolutely nothing on invites (by doing it via email, Facebook or even Eventbrite), or you can spend an absolute fortune on swanky invites by Smythson or the like. A card invitation is very special, but unless you are planning a huge party or celebration, I wouldn't spend your money on cards. I have written a little more on this in the Weddings chapter, as there are dedicated websites for inviting guests to weddings, but for a party the internet, in some shape or form, is in my view your best bet. Once you've compiled your guest list in Excel you can mail everyone from there – but don't forget to 'bcc' your guests or mail them individually, unless you don't mind them all seeing each other's email addresses.

Choose Food

Once upon a time it was easy to choose food and drink for a birthday party, or indeed any party. You bought (or if you were really talented – made) some vol-au-vents, egg and cress sarnies, provided Twiglets and crisps, bought in some Party Sevens and decorated the room with streamers. Unfortunately, or perhaps fortunately, that just won't hit the spot these days. Now you must take into account food allergies, intolerances and other dietary requirements, as well as religious and ethical dimensions. But there are four simple rules which faint-hearted party organisers can live by:

1. Chicken is the least offensive meat.

2. Salad is your gluten-free friend – provided you don't add croutons (no Caesars, then).

3. A sponge cake is a nut-free must-have.

4. People like standing.

Eh, what's Number 4 got to do with the price of fish? Well, what it means is that you can go canapés and bowl food rather than a sit-down if that's your preference, in the full knowledge that you won't be upsetting your guests. It gives them the freedom to move around and allows you to spend more on drink and less on food – result!

If you stick to rules 1 to 3, it shouldn't be too difficult to construct a food menu for your guests, including the nibbly bits. Nowadays, most savvy venues and caterers know their stuff when it comes to allergies and other dietary issues, but of course do check with them if you are concerned, particularly if it is a sit-down do.

And, to add interest, your food could be themed, as per your chosen colour scheme, but that might be a stretch too far for a faint-heart – perhaps it might be worth mentioning to the venue or caterer as it can add a bit of extra fun to the proceedings – you could go for a red velvet cake, a Black Forest gateau, beetroot (great with salmon, and actually you can add that to a cake too), goat's cheese with black crackers, pomegranate with most things these days...

Chose Drink

If you love drink, alcoholic or not, there has never been a better time to be alive. What an array of fantastic choices in wine, spirits, cocktails, aperitifs and digestifs there are, as well as amazing 'mocktails' and soft drinks. Just 20 or so years ago, your only non-alcoholic choice, apart from Coke, was warm Schweppes or Britvic orange or pineapple juice. So your choices are, like your venue choices, limited only by your imagination – and your budget. If your theme is Caribbean, you will want rum in your cocktails, or if you are going all 60s, you might want Babycham – yes, it's still available!

But if you are having a simple non-themed birthday party, wine and spirits are what's required, along with an attractive non-alcoholic alternative.

On costs: unfortunately, this is where the venue knows its onions and will want to charge you quite a lot for a simple house wine – and the house wines are not always that great, so if you can afford it, it might be best to up your game and pay a little extra for something better. It depends on what you think your guests will like – you don't want them all rushing to buy their own bottles from the venue's bar. But depending on your budget (and you can put this in the invitation and/or menu at the venue) you could have a cash bar after the first round of drinks – that way, those who don't want wine but would rather have beer or cocktails can get their own and you don't end up spending an absolute fortune.

And on the topic of how much to order: most venues use smaller glasses than they would offer at the bar, so you can bank on around 5-6 glasses per standard bottle of wine. I've seen some estimates that say people will drink around one glass an hour, but I think it depends entirely on the type of party. If it's a sit-down, possibly, but if it's a reception, they may drink more. Whichever way you slice it, drink will be pricey, which is why, if you are going for an external venue, it might be best to go for a cash bar at some point so you don't get a nasty surprise when the bill arrives.

Choose Content

A birthday party can be as simple as having some friends round, eating and drinking, maybe playing a game and playing music on your iPod – oh, and maybe someone will get the guitar out and have a strum and a bit of a singalong. Or it could be a swing from the chandeliers type party with chocolate fountains, Butlers in the Buff and cocktails agogo. Or anything in between. Usually it has elements of the first two, if not the third. But as you're time poor and just thinking about adding content to a party makes you feel faint, then try thinking about it this way:

What do you want your guests to do at the party for the majority of the time: eat, drink, gas, dance? If that's all you want, then all you need to add to your food and drink are either an iPod or Spotify and some speakers, or if you've got the space and you're minted, is that even a word?, a DJ. But if you want something a bit different, memorable perhaps, more personal to you and your guests maybe, more exciting, more exotic, well, there are lots of different types of entertainment, from a LED hula hoop performer to a magician, from a quiz to a comedian, or for a really fantastic finale, fireworks. Then there are games, like charades, Twister, Jenga, table football (yes, you can hire the table), bucking bronco, Gladiator game, giant chess...the list is almost endless. Or do you want to push the boat out and hire some Strictly stars to teach your guests to Salsa?

A great way to get guests to mingle, particularly at a significant birthday party where you may have friends and relatives from different parts of the country or the world and who may not all know each other, is to hold a quiz. Now I don't mean the sit-down variety you would get at your local pub, butone that starts and finishes within the party and is designed to get people to mingle. So, how do you do that? Well, you make it all about you! Write up 20 questions about yourself. Each question should be able to be answered by at least one or more of the guests – so, for example, you could ask the name of the school you attended, or your first pet's name, the title of your first job, or where you met your partner, so that a guest from each time of your life will at least know the answer to one of those questions. And those that don't will have to find relevant people within the party to get the answers – simples! And you could offer a bottle of bubbly or some choccies for the winner – it's a great ice breaker and can help to prevent little cliques of guests forming.

Dress, Dress, Dress Dress the Room

Yes, you could just blow up a few cursory balloons and tie them with some streamers, but it's your birthday - you want to make it a bit special, don't you? So, depending on your chosen theme or your room's colour scheme, how can you add a bit of pizzazz? Balloons are a great way to pretty up a room and nowadays you can get hold of some great shaped balloons made of unusual materials, not just the classic matt or shiny finish, but ones that look more like cloth and are larger and have more impact than bog standard party balloons. And, best of all, you can get them filled with helium and weighted if necessary, so all you have to do is place them.

Flowers, of course, add decoration to an event. Again, depending on your theme, you can go vintage and use mason jars (just another word for old fashioned jam jars), or get some elaborate floral arrangements made, or anything in between. As a faint-heart, I would opt for using a florist rather than doing it myself and a good florist can be creative within most people's budgets, coming up with simple or more complex ideas depending on what you want. And if you don't know what you want, but you have picked the venue, the florist should be able to give you some ideas of what will work in that space.

Lighting can play an important part in a party – too light and you won't create atmosphere, too dark and you can't see your guests. A mixture of uplighters and tea lights works well, depending on the room, so you don't need anything elaborate, but there are some amazing options should your budget stretch, from garlands and arches to LED votives.

Then there is draping, chair coverings, tablecloths, napkins and centrepieces ... all these elements will make your event memorable, but they are not essentials but extras, which if you have the time and the inclination, can add to the atmosphere.

In terms of layout, I think it's nice to have a mixture of sizes and seats – sofas for lolling, poser tables for posing (your drinks and nibbles, as well as yourself!), some chairs and low tables, unless you are having a sit-down meal, in which case you could devise a table plan or just let people sit where they want – that's what I did at my wedding for 60 guests. And, if at all possible, if your venue has a lot of hard surfaces, see if there is any way they can dampen those a little because once the room is filled with people, the decibel level will rise considerably and you may have to shout to each other over the general din.

Pick a Photographer and/or Photo Booth and/or Videographer

Yes, I know everyone takes photos these days on their phones, so you might question why you need a professional photographer rather than your cousin's best friend or your children. But trust me, if you are having a special event like a significant birthday, you want to be sure that it's been recorded by someone who knows what they are doing. Nowadays, photography is all about reportage, so less posed and more natural – but you will still want to have some photos of you and your family and/or friends, so you'll need to gather the relevant people together for these at some point during the evening, probably after the food but before the cake. It is an added expense, but so worth it for the memories – so many of us love Facebook and looking back over photos we've uploaded over the years, as well as having tangible images we can frame.

Another recent trend is to provide polaroid cameras for your guests that they can then use to take pictures – and you can hang a line up somewhere within the party with pegs on which the images can dry - the great thing about Polaroids is their immediacy, but they do have a tendency to fade, so they are fine as an add-on but I wouldn't rely on them as a main recorder of the event.

Using a videographer can be a great idea too, particularly if you ask them to interview guests as well as filming them. It can be quite difficult to find videographers, as photographers don't often provide a videographer service as well as photography, but wedding supplier websites should be a good first port of call.

A photo booth can be a lot of fun – if you haven't seen one before, it's a portable version of the old style photo booth that you used when you needed the dreaded passport photo, only with silly hats! They only work, though, if you have guests who are up for going in and having silly pictures taken, and I wouldn't use them as a substitute for a proper photographer or videographer.

Plan Timings

Most parties tend to start at 7.30/8pm and finish at 12/1am, particularly if they are held at a designated venue rather than a private house – although even in someone's house or apartment you don't want to annoy the neighbours too much with endless karaokes of 'Dancing Queen' and 'Hi Ho Silver Lining' after midnight – unless they have been invited. But what is key to a successful event is how it will flow. What do I mean by that? Well, from the time the guests arrive to the time they leave, it's a good idea to have a notion of what they will do and what will happen at certain stages throughout the evening. Yes, you could just put them in a room with food, drink and music and let them get on with it, so to speak, but does that make for a good party? It depends what you think your guests will enjoy. If they want a good old catch-up and there is seating enough for them to spend the evening doing that, then that's fine, but in my experience guests want a bit more. After all, they have bothered to get dressed up, maybe brought a present for the party girl or boy, maybe trekked halfway across London or on country roads to get to the venue, so when they get there, do they just want to stand around with a plate in one hand, a glass in the other, chewing the cud? It's particularly difficult with people you don't know, trying to make conversation over music and trying to think of something interesting to ask the other person that isn't the inevitable 'do you live locally' or 'and what do you do'? So, as suggested above, some content is a good idea. And once you've decided on content, you need to think about when you'd like it to happen. So, rough timings for a birthday party with, say, a magician and a DJ might look like this:

8pm Guests arrive, given welcome drink, proceed to nibble table (not literally!), chat. Background music plays. Photographer snaps away.

8.30pm Magician circulates amongst the guests.

9pm Magician stops, food is served or laid on table for self-service. 9.45pm DJ begins, encourages guests to dance.

10.15pm Birthday cake is brought, speech and candles are blown out. Photographer finishes. 10.30pm to midnight Dancing

12 midnight Carriages

That is a very simple timeline or event flow. If you add games, you might have them available to play all evening until the dancing, say.

This kind of event flow is helpful for all the suppliers you use, such as the venue manager, caterer, and photographer, as well as any entertainer, so they know when to bring out the champers for toasting, or for when the photographer needs some group shots. If everyone knows where they need to be at what time, it will help the event run smoothly.

Record It All on a Spreadsheet

Argh – a spreadsheet – what is this, a piece of work? Well, a party is work, or at least the preparation is, and sometimes even the event itself. So, in order to make less work for yourself, so that you know who is doing what, who you've booked, how much it's all going to cost, who needs paying and when, what the cancellation period and fees are (check the contract you may have to sign with the venue and/or suppliers), it really makes sense to record all your transactions on a spreadsheet. Then you can see at a glance what the hell is going on. You probably do this in your working life so you might as well do it for your party – after all, you are spending your hard-earned cash on a blowout and you want it to go well. And you can also use a tab within that spreadsheet for the guest list and replies.

Get set and Party!

You've done all the prep and now it's the day of the party. So get your hair, make-up and nails done, or manicure and wet shave and beard trim, don your glad rags and away you go. Events have their own momentum, so once guests start arriving it should all go smoothly, as long as there is food, drink and people out for a good time!

2 WEDDINGS – THE GOOD, THE BAD AND THE BEAUTIFUL

This book isn't for 20- or even 30-somethings who want the whole nine yards, so if you're looking for a book that will help you organise a wedding at the Ritz for 500 guests, with a carriage pulled by six white horses, roses flown in from Argentina and a performance by Rihanna, put this book down immediately and maybe see a shrink. But if you want to organise a wedding for up to 300 people, in the UK or abroad, keep reading – after all, a wedding is simply an event that has a bit more content to it. It's a party with an add-on – the ceremony – which nowadays, depending on your religion or lack thereof, you can have all in one place. So whether you are the bride or groom, or a pair of either, or parents of one or the other, or a friend wanting to help out, read on.

Planning a wedding can be a tricky affair, particularly if you have a large or complicated family. In my experience, the best way to navigate potentially choppy seas is to be very clear about what you as a couple want before you start to discuss it with family and friends. That way there should be no arguments, no 'oh, but what about inviting Aunt Margaret' or 'but John will have to sit at the top table because...'. Following my simple Seventeen Steps to a Successful Wedding below will ensure you've thought of absolutely everything necessary to ensure you and your guests have the best time with the minimum of fuss.

Budget

As with any event, the size of your budget will determine what type of wedding you can expect to have. In 2015 the average cost of a wedding was £21,000, not including the honeymoon. That is a lot of dosh to splash out in one fell swoop, but for that spend you can have a fabulous and memorable event. The breakdown of that total includes around £10,000 just for the ceremony and venue. But you don't need to spend anything like that if you are not so inclined. Civil ceremonies cost around £115 at your local town hall and you can hire a room in a decent pub for around £1500 minimum spend (London price – outside London should be cheaper), so once you factor in a photographer, flowers and a DJ, as well as outfits, rings and a honeymoon, you could get away with around £5K or less.

A word on venues: some budget wedding guides suggest not letting a venue know that you will be celebrating a wedding, as they rack up their prices for weddings and civil partnerships. My advice is not to do that because you are going to have to continue with this dissembling throughout the whole event, as well as beforehand, as your contract with the venue may be null and void if they find out you've been fibbing, so it really isn't worth the fear and hassle in my view.

Guests and Invitations

Oh dear, I hear you cry - this is going to be a toughie! Well, it needn't be with me to hold your hand. Firstly, the venue – and the budget – will decide your guest numbers. Secondly, keep in mind that this is your day, not your cousin's, your stepmum's, your aunty in Australia's or your first cousin once removed's – it's all about you, your husband or wife-to-be, or partner, and the people you love. And if those people love you, they won't care if their relatives aren't invited – honest! And if they do, eff 'em! Seriously, you must get your priorities right. This is your day, and you want the people around you that love you and want to share the love with, so to speak. Not some add-ons who aren't sure exactly who you are or how they are related to you.

So, sit down with your partner – and allocate a good hour and half to two hours for this – and go through your guest list. Yes, it probably will be a bit tricky, but once done, you'll feel a whole lot better. And stick to it – don't be tempted to add one or two extras – try to be really comprehensive at the start, which probably means going through your Google contacts or fishing out old address books, or checking your Facebook friends, just to make sure you haven't forgotten someone vital – believe me, in these crazy busy days, it happens! So, guest list done and dusted – tick.

Actually, there is one thing I haven't mentioned – kids! Now it may be that you already have children with your partner or from a previous relationship and they may be under 16, in which case you may be happy to have children at your wedding. But some couples prefer their weddings to be child-free zones, particularly if they are under 10, so you may want to consider this when choosing guests, venue and timings. If you really want or have to have children present, consider a separate table for them at the reception and some space for them to let off steam – i.e. run around and play without being disruptive – experienced venues will be able to suggest how this can be accommodated.

Now for the Venue

As with other events, securing the venue should be your number one priority after you've worked out your guest list. Venues that hold civil ceremonies charge more – sometimes a lot more – than simple venues and the charges go up at weekends, so if you want to keep costs lower, go for a separate ceremony (e.g. town hall, church, synagogue etc.) and then proceed to the venue.

A long lead time (12-18 months) will help you to secure the venue you want.

If you have no idea where to start looking for your venue, there are many venue-finding services online that can help you. They can deal directly with clients or with their event planners, and can shortlist venues and arrange viewings. As a faint-heart, a venue-finding service (along with an event planner, natch) is your friend, as they can take the time and stress out of spending hours on the net surfing venues that often resolutely refuse to give you much detail on, for example, how many people it can seat or how much it will be on a Friday as compared to a Saturday, or how much their packages start at, so you will at some point have to visit the venues. But think laterally – if you are on a budget, a room in a pub can be made to look beautiful with some strategically placed balloons, flowers and bunting.

Invitations

Wedding invitations can cause many an argument. Even the wording, given the number of parents and step-parents to consider these days, can be a pain to agree. There are several wedding websites in the UK (Google them) that you can use to send your Save the Date invites – vital to ensure everyone gets the date in their diaries long before you send out the hard copy invitations, which I recommend you do. You do not need to spend a fortune on invitations – repeat after me – YOU DO NOT NEED TO SPEND A FORTUNE ON INVITATIONS. Yes, it is boring having to handwrite them, but honestly, you can design something online and get a printer to print them or use a specialist firm, but do keep it simple. You don't need an RSVP card; simply ensure that you've given every guest a date by which they must RSVP and chase them if they haven't – keep a note on your spreadsheet. As long as you've sent a Save the Date Email, you won't need to send your invitations out earlier than 2- 3 months before the date of the wedding.

Food and Drink

As with any party or event, your food and drink choices will be dictated by your budget. And as with any party, if the food isn't as important to you as, say, the wine, there is no need to splash out on Tournedos Rossini for your main – go for chicken with a veggie option, and choose something other than the house reds and whites. Unfortunately, most venues charge a lot more for wine than you would pay in Majestic or Tesco, so it is worth asking what corkage they would charge and bringing in your own – do the sums as it may work out cheaper for you to do this.

The length and timings of the wedding party will dictate

when and what food you choose. For example, if you have the wedding ceremony in the late afternoon, then the wedding feast at around 6pm, and you then plan to have dancing later on, you may want some nibbles at around 10 or 11pm, to keep your guests going until 2am. But if you are starting early and finishing early, say ceremony at 11am, feast at 1.30pm, and finishing at 4, with no evening do, then you are unlikely to need any extra nosh. To give you an idea of how much a caterer would cost, if you using a room above a pub, for example, or someone's private house, you will probably pay a minimum of £15 a head for canapés and bowl food outside London and maybe twice that or more inside the capital. For faint-hearts, if you can bear the cost, I would choose a caterer over friends or family any day. Just check them out first, ask for a tasting, ask for testimonials and actually contact the people who wrote them, then you should be sure of a super spread.

Décor

How you choose to decorate your room will depend as much on the venue itself as the budget you have to spend. If, for example, you choose a venue that has beautiful original features, such as cornicing, architraves and a feature fireplace, and with large windows overlooking a garden, you can enhance those features using minimal wedding decorations. But if you have a room above a pub that is bare and dark, you can liven it up with drapes, balloons and colour to make it warm and welcoming. As a faint-heart you may want to delegate the decoration to a friend who has the time and/or the inclination to help you. After all, do you have time to scour Pinterest for ideas?

Cake

For some couples, cake is the most important part of the

wedding feast, but for others, it's often an afterthought, particularly if they don't have a sweet tooth! Nowadays, wedding cakes can take many forms, from elaborate, traditionally-iced creations through naked, un-iced sponges, to cheese towers. And with gluten and sugar-free diets abounding, good cake makers are getting savvy with their baking and can cater for most tastes. The towers of power you see in magazines can look stunning, but make sure that you choose a cake that will fit in with the rest of the décor and room dressing. A cake maker recently told me that she was working with a bride who was most insistent on the colour of the cake and the rose petals that were to adorn it, but when the cake maker arrived to deliver the cake, the table on which it was to be placed was covered with orange tinged petals whereas the cake had pink tinged ones – ok, you might say, so what? But the bride was not happy and this was because she had failed to inform the venue of the colour of the cake's petals so a clash of colours occurred.

Booking the Wedding – the Official Bit

Once you have the venue secured, you can book your registry office, church or other place of worship. With a registry office wedding or civil partnership, you must give at least 28 full days' notice at your local register office. You need to include details of where you intend to get married or form a civil partnership. Your notice will be publicly displayed in the register office for 28 days. And don't do what I did and take it to the wire, then get stuck in a traffic jam on the way and be met by a snotty civil servant telling me that as we'd missed the slot we might not get another appointment for weeks, too late for the actual wedding to be officiated at! You may also need to give notice here if you plan to marry or form a civil partnership abroad. Ask the overseas authority if you'll need a 'certificate of no impediment'. You can only give notice at a register office if you have lived in the registration district for at least the past 7 days. In England and Wales, a registry office wedding costs £119 altogether. Notice must be given at least 16 days in advance. You'll also need at least two witnesses. A church wedding is more expensive and the fee is £413. The Church of England's special wedding site explains: 'There is a required legal fee for marrying in a church. If you marry outside your own parish, it is £486 in 2015'. You don't usually need to give notice with the register office if you're getting married in an Anglican church and both you and your partner are British citizens or from the European Economic Area or Switzerland. Other religions will have their own requirements. Jewish and Quaker marriages: officials performing Jewish or Quaker marriages will register marriages. For marriages in other religions, it's best to ask the minister or officiator concerned. The British Government website has comprehensive info on all of the above, so if in doubt, check it out.

Timings

These will need to be considered along with the choice of venue. For example, the venue might cost a lot less in the daytime, so you could decide to have a morning ceremony, civil or religious, followed by lunch and finish at around 4pm. This will be considerably cheaper than holding the wedding in the evening, particularly at weekends. Some weddings start in the early afternoon, are followed by a late lunch for the closest guests, then there is a hiatus until the evening when more guests are invited to join in the evening celebrations. It all depends on your venue, your preference and your purse.

Ceremony

A wedding is made up of two parts, which are the Declatory and the Contracting Words. The Declatory Words: These words are at the start of the ceremony and must be included. The Declatory Words are: I do solemnly declare that I know not of any lawful impediment why I [name] may not be joined in matrimony to [name].

The Contracting Words: These are the legal words that marry you and these feature towards the end of the ceremony. The Contracting Words are: I call upon these persons here present, to witness that I [name] do take thee [name] to be my lawful wedded wife / wife - husband / husband.

Additional words can be added before or after the Contracting Words to complete your wedding vows. There are no legal words that need to be said when forming a civil partnership. Most ceremonies do, however, include the following paragraph that can be included at any point in the ceremony: I declare that I know not of any legal reason why we may not register as partners in law. I understand that on signing this document we will be forming a civil partnership with each other.

Most local councils' websites will have information on what they can offer in addition to the standard wording. For example, Haringey Council in London offers a choice of three wedding 'scripts' for marriages and civil partnerships, with templates for you to insert your own choice of words. Depending on what's on offer, and the space and time allowed by your local authority, you could even have a song or a poem. Friends who were getting married after being together for forty years decided that the bride would enter the room to the song 'At Last' by Etta James! If you are having your civil ceremony in a venue, you will have a lot more time to spend on the ceremony itself, and can choose songs, poems and music to suit your particular taste.

So, you've got your venue, you've booked your date with the register office at your local council (and by the way, if the venue is in a different area to the one where you live, your local authority will send the details they have taken from you at your appointment to the appropriate authority for that venue – but you'll need to book the local authority near the venue first). And now comes the fun bit!

Content

Now you can start to plan all the other wonderful accoutrements, such as food, drink, music, photographer, videographer, transport, décor, dress, suit, flowers, favours – need to lie down?! Look, you don't need to make a wedding complicated – it is, after all, just a party, albeit with a ceremony attached. But it is also a public celebration of your love for your partner, something you may well only do once in your life, or this may be the second, third or fourth time you are doing it, but whatever stage in life you're at, it is a very special event and you want it to reflect you and your partner's values.

So what makes a memorable wedding, or even any event, for that matter? Well, something that stimulates the five senses. So if you get it right, you and your guests will experience memorable sights, tastes, aromas, touches and sounds that will stay with them long after the event has passed. Now you might think that, as a faint-heart, do I really have time for this, but honestly, you do!

Think about a Halloween party you've been to, for example. That will have touched at least some of your senses if it was done well. You'll have seen and felt cobwebs, you'll have heard ghoulish cries, you'll have tasted nibbles with the texture of eyeballs, and you may have inhaled something akin to eye of newt and toe of frog. Now of course your wedding will be nothing like that, unless you and your partner are Goths, but what you can do is tickle the five senses in the same way. So here are some ideas to get your juices flowing, so to speak!

Visuals

The easiest way to pretty up a room and make it a visual feast is to decorate it with flowers. Centrepieces on the tables and the odd display dotted about will add some pizzazz to any room. I mentioned balloons earlier, and if you choose a few strategically placed ones, or an arrangement such as a garland or trees, they can add to the visual feast of the event.

Table Plan and Layout

Eek, the table plan – who should sit where? Will Uncle Jack sit next to Cousin Ivan because they haven't spoken for 20 years but it's the only place we can put him because Cousin Betty is related to...? OMG! You can only do what you can do, as they say, so if they have to sit next to each other, so be it – they will have to put aside their disagreements for this, your special day. Top tables can be a pain, as the couple gets stuck next to an in-law – great if you get on but a drag if you don't – so you could consider using a circular table as the 'top table' – the only issue with this is to ensure that all guests can see the speechmakers who traditionally sit there. Otherwise, I don't see it as a problem. Just make sure you give the venue the table plan and guest list in advance so they can pop it up at the room's entrance so people know where to head for.

Sounds

I do think it's hard to beat live music. It doesn't have to be a full band, maybe just a guitar and voice, or a piano (many venues have their own), but at least early on in the event some live music really adds something special, especially a wedding where the emphasis is on the romantic. After the meal and speeches, DJs are perfectly in order, but do make sure you tell him or her what your musical preferences are, as you may not want to find that the Birdie Song is his/her idea of a dancefloor hit! Or if the venue allows, and they often do these days, bring your iPod or give them your Spotify login details and you can listen to your own playlists. If you find that some of your preferred bands, musicians or DJs are booked up, you could think laterally and find a rock choir or an acapella group, particularly if you're not having dancing.

Touch, Tastes, Scents

Ok, in an event guide for faint-hearts, it's not really appropriate to delve into the senses in too much detail, but depending on your theme, you could feed touch by decorating the room in velvet or linen, tickle the taste buds with unusual flavours and textures, and scent the venue with heady fragrances. All these will add to your guests' enjoyment and make the event all the more memorable.

Speeches

Ah, speeches! Honestly, there is no need to stress! Firstly, I think both parties should make speeches – to hell with convention, this day belongs to both of you, so why shouldn't you both say something if you want to. And secondly, you really don't have to write them up beforehand. No one cares if they're funny or sad – let me tell you, it's much worse having to sit through some boring drone-on reading from a bit of paper with no delivery and no pitch. What your guests want to hear is how happy you are on this special day and how even more happy you are that they have joined you in celebrating it. That's all – end of. But, of course, if you want to be funny and do a routine, or sing a song or whatever, it's your day and you should do as you please. I just want to reassure you that guests will not expect a Ted Talk!

Recap

So, let's recap: we've got our venue, our service, our timings, and we are considering content. The food and drink can wait until nearer the time – if you are using the venue's in-house caterers – although if you have to bring in catering from outside it's a good idea to start sourcing them, as the good ones will get very booked up, particularly over the summer, the most popular time for weddings. But once you've chosen your caterer, you won't need to worry about choosing food and drink until a couple of months or so before the wedding.

Photographer

But what you will need to do once venue and timings have been sorted is pick and book your photographer. The best ones are really in demand and can get booked up to a year, or even eighteen months, in advance. Photographers are a great bunch of people and very supportive of each other in my experience. If they are busy and can't do a job, they will suggest others who may be available – this has happened to me several times – so don't be too despondent if you don't get your first choice. Have a good look at their website and their ethos so you know the type of weddings he or she usually does, and whether they tend to do traditional wedding posing or more reportage, which is the fashion nowadays. You will pay a considerable amount for wedding photographs – the cost is in the presentation, as you will be offered various options such as on a CD, in a 'digital' book, in frames – the list goes on and on. Prices start at around £500 and can rise to £2,000 or more – it all depends on what you want to end up with, as well as the standard and experience of your photographer. It is well worth getting at least three quotes and comparing and contrasting what you get for the money.

Favours or Guest Gifts

I think favours have fallen out of favour – excuse the pun – as they are seen as an unnecessary extravagance. But if you want to give your guests a takeaway pressie, you can either spend a few bob, say £16 or so, for a personalised scented candle, or go low and buy choccies at around £2 a pop but the catch is you have to buy a minimum order of 100. Or you could pop to your local pound shop to see if you can find a tiny wee pressie – but even still, that is £150 to £200 for something that will probably get lost on the way home.

So we've covered budget, ceremony, guests, venue, and content. The only thing we haven't mentioned is the honeymoon, but that's not really within the remit of this book. All you need to consider once you've booked the wedding, if you are planning to shoot off the following morning, is that you've got a room. Then it's like any other holiday, but you don't need me to tell you that!

3 CELEBRATIONS – FESTIVALS, FEASTS AND FESTIVITIES

Christmas, New Year, Halloween, Bonfire Night, Burns Night, St Patricks Day, other religious celebrations

Christmas and other day celebration parties, in some ways, are easier to organise or at least to populate with decorations and food, as the occasion itself already has rituals and must-do's that guests expect. So, for example, where would a Christmas party be without mince pies and mulled wine? A Bonfire Night without baked potatoes? Or a Burns Night without haggis? Of course, you don't have to have any of those things at your celebration, but it is helpful to know what has gone before, so to speak, so you don't have to spend hours agonising over whether to decorate the room in green for St Patrick's Day (correct) or mull over whether to score the odd pumpkin for Bonfire Night (no, that's the week before). If you belong to a particular religion, you will already know what content is required for your celebration party, so I won't be going into those here, but most celebration parties have four things in common:

They will usually include a ritual – e.g. an Address to the Haggis on Burns Night, setting off fireworks in the garden for Bonfire Night, or singing Auld Lang Syne at midnight for the New Year's Eve party.

A particular type of food will be served.

Particular music will be played – yes, that probably means Bing or Michael Bublé at Christmas, or the Irish Rover at a St Patrick's Day party.

And most importantly, they are usually held in someone's home. That's not to say you can't hold it at an external venue, but most people choose to have this type of party in their home – so this will involve more work on your part, as there will be all that clearing up to do afterwards!

So, what can a faint-heart do to minimise work and cost? Well, taking the four common elements above, let's see what we can do to minimise your workload:

Identify one or two close friends to be in charge of the ritual – so if it's Burns Night, ask your Scottish friend to agree to do the Address to the Haggis, and maybe even bring it to the party, so you don't have to think about the ritual. Or on Bonfire Night, designate a friend or two as firework gurus and get them to come early, place the fireworks strategically in the garden, and give them the task of setting them off at an appropriate time.

Ask your friends to bring the relevant food, so designate one friend to bring the mince pies, say, or the colcannon if it's St Patrick's Day, and make sure you make a list so you know who's bringing what – otherwise you'll end up with

250 mince pies and nothing savoury.

Designate someone to be DJ and bring the appropriate music on their iPod or that they've created a playlist on Spotify.

If the party is to be held at your home, ask a couple of close friends if they will help you to set up – e.g. prepare the pumpkins or decorate the house with Christmas bunting before the party, and have another couple to help with binning the rubbish and washing-up at the end – you can tempt them with a special seasonal pressie or drink next time you go out.

If you follow those four steps, your faint-hearted quotient will be significantly reduced and you can enjoy the party without that nagging thought at the back of your mind about how much mess everyone is making and how long it will take to clear up.

4 CORPORATE – AWARDS, AWAY DAYS, ASSEMBLIES

Once upon a time, I worked as a professional charity fundraiser at various charities, including Breakthrough Breast Cancer (now part of Breast Cancer Now), Ovarian Cancer Action and Working Families. At Breakthrough, I had the most wonderful job – it was my task to ask our supporters to organise balls, quizzes and dinners for the charity – and I will come on to those in the next chapter. So no fundraising events for me in that role. But what I did have to do was organise corporate away weekends, or weekend workshops as we called them, around the country, where we would invite those very committed supporters who themselves organised regular events for the charity to a weekend in a corporate environment, so they could learn more about the charity's work and then go out and advocate for the cause. They were so much fun, those weekends, as it was a chance to say thank you to those committed women and men who gave up so much of their free time to the charity and made a real difference to people affected by this dreadful disease.

So, there may come a time in a faint-heart's life when you will have to organise an away weekend, or a launch party, or an award ceremony – particularly popular now - or even a conference. It may be that you are a PA in a corporate environment, or working in PR, or even for a charity, and you've never organised a corporate-style event in your life. Well, that was me when I started at Breakthrough – the largest party or event I'd ever organised was for 50 people in my own home. So when I was tasked with planning an away weekend at Breakthrough, I must admit I did panic slightly! However, as with the Celebration chapter, there are four fundamentals that are common to all corporate-style events that should be followed, and which should help you to plan a successful and engaging event – sorry, corporate speak alert – so that your attendees feel they've had a great day, night or weekend.

The absolute must-have for a successful corporate event is a clear idea of what the event is designed to achieve. So, for example, is it to motivate employees, to better engage them? Is it for customers or clients to learn about your product? Or is it to reward top salespeople? If you have a clear objective for the event, the content will be easy to create.

Choose a venue that has good transport links. So, close to a tube or train station so that delegates or guests can get to it easily. The words 'eggs' and 'grandmother' may spring to mind here, but you'll find that in a corporate environment you will get sent lots of info on out-of-the-way venues that have great day delegate rates or are very reasonably priced, but which are impossible to get to or from unless you have a car.

Choose a venue which has in-house or easy access to audio visual (AV) equipment. If you have to start bringing in your own, this will increase the cost – particularly if you have to have someone there to operate it, so this will probably mean a more modern venue, maybe a rather boring one like a hotel rather than an attractive unusual space, which may look great but lack the modern facilities needed to make a corporate event a success.

And finally, make sure it has good disabled access. Venues are supposed to have this by law, but there are exemptions so do check this, as a responsible corporate will want to ensure it is seen to be taking diversity and inclusion seriously.

If it's a conference you are organising, ask your venue what their day delegate rate is, which is the cost for one person to spend a day at the venue and which should include tea, coffee, water and lunch. Depending on numbers, you can often negotiate a better rate than the original 'rack' (standard) rate, particularly if some delegates will need to stay the night.

Now, it could be that you are a trainer or coach and you want to organise a seminar or training session. These can be quite daunting if you've never done one before, as you may be concerned that no one will sign up or turn up and you've laid out all this money on a venue, prettying it up, preparing training materials or a fantastic speech, then three women and a dog pitch up expecting you to give them your all. Which you will, won't you, even if you've only got a few people in attendance? But...if you want to be sure that you get bums on seats, so to speak, follow the steps outlined earlier in this chapter about setting objectives and being clear what knowledge your participants will take away from the event. Then you can start sending out your marketing materials and hopefully attracting attendees.

But how big or small a venue should I book, I hear you cry, and what if no one comes? The best advice I can give you is this:

Set the event up on Eventbrite – and point all your contacts to that page – don't set it up on Facebook as well, as it may confuse attendees and you, as you struggle to match the Facebook names with those on Eventbrite. Or just use Facebook – but I think Eventbrite looks more professional and is easier to administer – and a must if you are charging a ticket price.

Find your venue – ask your contacts or use a venue-finding service, and find out whether you have to pay in advance, what the cancellation policy is and what's included in the price. If money is tight, look for venues that have a basement in use only at night – so a club, for example, might be happy to let you have an unused room for nothing, if you are getting bums on seats ordering drinks or sandwiches.

Sit back and pray!

5 CHARITY FUNDRAISING – DINNERS, QUIZZES, BALLS ETC.

People love a charity fundraiser! What could be better than trotting along to an event, getting all dolled up, partnering up with some mates, and knowing you're going to have a great time AND help a deserving charity? So, as the organiser of such an event, you've got a head start. Well, up to a point. As with a corporate event, your most important starting point is to work out what you are trying to achieve – and usually this will usually be expressed in lots of £ signs.

So, how are you going to maximise income with keeping expenditure low? Well, let's take the classic example of a charity quiz evening. This need not cost a bomb, as you can use a room in a pub for a very small layout – sometimes nothing at all as you will be bringing punters into the venue – and then all you need is a quiz writer and presenter (sometimes one and the same person) who may well do it for nothing or at least a very small fee (to give you an example, the charity rate of an excellent quiz duo is at the time of writing £250 – and they give good quiz!), some food and a prize or two, perhaps donated by the pub itself or a local business. You can also maximise income on the night by asking businesses to provide raffle prizes. A faint-heart shouldn't find this too onerous a task, particularly if you can rope in a friend or three to help you.

Most pub quizzes charge £1 a person or so for entry, but as this is for charity £5 isn't too steep. But that is not going to bring in much needed revenue for the charity, unless you have 10 tables of 6 all paying £5 – but even with my maths that's only £300, which is a tidy sum but won't keep most charities afloat for more than about five minutes. If you want to make serious money for your charity, you will have to pay out some of what you would pay for a regular event – but hopefully not all. For example, your venue should offer a charity rate, which should be at least 20% lower than the regular rate. So you might find your minimum spend on a venue goes down from say £4K to £3200 on a venue holding around 150 people – this is a central London price, by the way, so outside of London you should pay a lower price – and this should include food, although not drink. So then you could price your ticket at £50 (£50 x 150 = £7,500 minus £3,200) making a profit of £4,300 on the ticket price alone. Adding in the cost of a welcome Prosecco might take your costs up to £3,200 plus£750 = £3,950, but that will still give you a very good profit of £3,550.

But what are you going to do to attract people to your charity event? If people are going to pay £50 a ticket, and usually they come as a pair, they will want added value – a speaker, an entertainer, a karaoke maybe. If it's your first ever fundraiser, start with a quiz – but give it a twist – it could be seasonal or topical – something that takes it above the ordinary. That will ensure you should get a good take-up and raise lots of money for your good cause. And a big pat on the back for doing it!

Now, it may be that your organisation is short of money. So you will have to improvise, if, for example, your budget doesn't run to flowers. At an event I organised at the House of Lords, we put coloured tissue paper in plain glass vases and prettied it up so that the paper could have been mistaken for flowers. Ok, well, not really mistaken, but they did look effective and at least we had some pretty things to put on the poser tables. Other ideas you could use for jollying up a bare looking room include bunting (not at the House of Lords, LOL), Christmas lights, tea lights and ribbons. Guests tend to be a lot more forgiving of a hand-knitted look as long as you have been seen to have made an effort and given them as much added value as you can, by being incredibly welcoming, giving them great content and thanking them profusely, not just at the event, but afterwards. And on that note, do try to get your guests' contact details so you can send them a thank you email, and to let them know about future fundraisers.

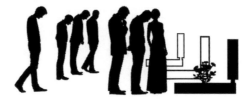

6 FUNERALS – COMMISERATIONS AND COMMEMORATIONS

Terribly gloomy, I know, but we all have to go sometime, and funerals can be an opportunity for family and friends who maybe haven't seen each other in years to get together. No one is saying hang out the bunting, but it is worth saying something about how to organise a funeral – or the post funeral get-together, particularly if you haven't attended one before, or your family member hasn't left instructions on what they want to happen – which is probably most of us, I'm guessing. The first funeral I attended was a friend's aged just 30, and the next was my mother's, when I was 37. I was so devastated that I left everything to my stepfather, which I regret, and I didn't go back to their home with him afterwards. When my stepfather himself died a few months later, his brother asked us all to go back to his flat for a drink and a chat, and that's when I realised how important the post funeral party can be, because it's a chance to talk about the departed, share stories, laugh as well as cry together and in a safe space – snuffling in a cold church or other place of worship

– non-denominational alternatives are available – is no real comfort, but sitting together with people who care about the deceased can be quite cathartic.

Firstly, it will depend on your religion, or lack thereof, and whether there has to be an autopsy, and as to how long you have between death and the funeral. In the Jewish and Muslim religions, for example, burial usually takes place a day or two after death, but if you choose a C of E funeral, or a non-religious cremation, it could be a week or ten days before the service takes place. So you may have a very short period in which to organise something or there may at least be a few days in which to do it. Most people choose to hold a post funeral party in their own home, but nowadays there are many pubs, particularly of the gastro variety, which regularly open their doors to post funeral events in the daytime. There will usually be a minimum spend, but it may be a worthwhile layout as you won't have to worry about anything other than turning up. If you do it at home, it will be like any party in that you will have to serve the drinks and the food and make sure everyone has somewhere to sit, particularly if you have elderly rellies in attendance. Using a caterer might be the best option if you do decide to hold it in your home, as you can then tend to attendees who might be feeling emotionally raw and need some comfort. So these choices, as with all event planning, are budget dependent. Just rest assured that in this very stressful time, you should be able to find somewhere to accommodate you and your party post funeral.

7 LEGALS, RISK MANAGEMENT, INSURANCE AND CONTINENGY PLANS ...YAWN, BUT SKIP AT YOUR PERIL!

Argh, I hear you cry! As if I wasn't faint-hearted already, you want to hit me with legal stuff? And better yet, insurance? Don't worry, this is a very short chapter which could save you heartache and money. So please don't look away just yet.

Legals

Location and noise are the two factors with legal issues attached to them. With regard to location, it is vital to check whether you have permission from the owner of the property or land to hold the event in that location. If it's your own house, obv, or even a rented property, you should be fine (although you might want to double-check the lease just to be safe). But you may decide that your street would be a great place for a party – and increasingly street parties are proving very popular, not just for residents but also for businesses. I know of one business in central London that regularly organises a street party as a marketing and networking opportunity every summer. So if this is something you are considering doing – although faint-hearts might want to have a lie down in a darkened room before committing to this – you will need permission from the local authority, so make sure you secure that before committing to anything else, and certainly don't book or pay any suppliers until you know for certain you have that permission.

The other issue to consider from a legal perspective is noise or nuisance. If you are having your do at a recognised event space, no probs – that will all be sorted out for you. But if you are having it at home and say you are having a marquee, you'll be in the garden, you may have a DJ and/or live band, and are planning to make some noise after midnight, you should consider how you can keep your neighbours sweet, as the last thing you want is a bobby knocking on your door. So here are some top tips on ensuring you don't get a visit from Mr or Ms Plod during your party:

Unhelpfully, there isn't a decibel level at which noise becomes a statutory (i.e. legally defined) nuisance. The factors that are considered when deciding whether a noise is a nuisance and therefore might be legally actionable (i.e. you might be taken to court for making such a noise) are:

How loud it is.

Length of time it continues.

How often it occurs.

The time of day.

Where the noise is taking place.

The 'test' is based overall on what is reasonable for the ordinary person to expect.

So, quite frankly, if you are having a party on a Friday or Saturday night in a residential area, close to a town centre, you will probably be fine – although it is a good idea to let the neighbours know well in advance. If you live in a small village, you should definitely tell the neighbours, and maybe even invite them! But as long as you are sensitive to your environment and don't go on till the early hours say not past 2am – you should be fine. It is always a case of 'do as you would be done by' in my view.

A word on music – if you are playing live or recorded music in a venue, you should check that the venue has a licence – most venues do, but occasionally they don't, although they should have if they are playing music during the course of their business – i.e., when you want to hire them. So worth checking, particularly if you are a charity or a company, as you wouldn't want any adverse publicity attached to you if it was revealed you hadn't checked and had not done your due diligence.

Risk Management

Minimising risk at home

So, you've sorted out the venue, food and drink, timings, guest list and suppliers. Now run the whole event through from start to finish in your mind. If you're holding it at a private house, go from front of house to garden, imagining hordes of people tramping through, crowding in the kitchen or around the barbecue if you're having it outdoors, dogs, children, music, and general mayhem, and what impact each of those things could have. Again, if it's outdoors, where is your barbecue situated? Is it too near the neighbours' garden so they will have to put up with the smoke, or can you move it somewhere else, and if you do move it, what impact will that have on cooking and serving up? Do you have a water feature or pond that could be a hazard for young children?

What about fireworks? Is your garden big enough to accommodate setting them off, or do you have too many trees for it to be safe to set off Chinese lanterns?

Minimising Risk at a Venue

Any venue worth its salt should do this for you, but as a

responsible event organiser – yes, that means you – you should check that you are happy with the space and the way the event will flow, just as you would within your own home. Responsible venues should be aware of any risks, but for your own peace of mind, if something looks dodgy to you it probably is, so ask questions and don't be afraid of looking silly – you won't – and a good event manager within the venue will be absolutely fine with you asking probing questions about whether that dangling cable is safe or what their food hygiene scores on the doors are.

Insurance

Insurance? Why would I need that? Well, the answer is you probably don't, for if you're having the event in your own home, your contents policy should cover you for public liability insurance, which will cover you for accidents occurring to your guests, and similarly your venue should have their own. So, check your home contents insurance, that's it's up to date, that you've paid the premium, and then check that you have public liability insurance included within it. Most home contents insurance includes public liability, but do check and make sure it doesn't contain any exclusions, such as not covering you for BBQ or firework accidents. Your guests are what is termed 'lawful invitees', they have a right to be on your property because you have invited them, and as such are entitled to be protected from any hazards that may be lurking in your home or garden. The test for such hazards would be what the reasonable person would be expected to minimise and what precautions the reasonable person would take to minimise risks to their guests. But if you are using suppliers, e.g. caterers, marquee companies, musicians, magicians, DJs etc., you should check that they have their own public liability insurance, because if they don't and they cause an accident, someone else will have to pick up the bill – and that could be you.

Contingency Plans

So, you've planned to have a garden party, or any outdoor

party, and it rains – doesn't it always? So what can you do to ensure your outdoor party isn't spoiled because good old Blighty has tried to blight your event?

If you're using an external venue, talk to them about their contingencies – they will almost certainly have them. So, for example, do they have an awning or a canopy they can put over the outside space? If you have to come inside, will the room be prepared and dressed? If you are holding the event at your own home, you can't bring the BBQ indoors – no, seriously - so make sure you've thought about how you will manage if you have to cook indoors, if you're doing it yourself, or if you are using caterers, ask them what they do in such circumstances.

All these may seem blindingly obvious but it is worth adding them to do your 'To Do' List as questions to ask or consider.

8 USING AN EVENT PLANNER – WHY WOULD YOU?

There are many event, party and wedding planners out there all eager to get their hands on your event. But stop – before you consider using one, there are seven key questions you should ask of them before taking the plunge and booking them? These are they:

What is their speciality? If they are used to doing corporate events and you want a simple birthday party, they might not be for you. Check out past events on their website and read their testimonials to gauge whether they are the right fit.

What services do they offer? Do they provide the whole shebang, including on-the-day event management, or can you pick and choose from a range of offers?

What's included in their fee? It's really important to establish what their fees cover so there are no surprises. For example, do they charge extra for support staff?

Who will be working on your event? Will there be a team or just one, and is there back-up?

What technology do they use? What tools do they use to project manage the event, and if it's ticketed, do they use a platform like Eventbrite to manage the guest list and payment?

How will they protect your event? Do they have insurance, and do they check their third party suppliers have their own? What if it rains? What contingency plans do they have in place?

What is their cancellation and refund policy? If the event cannot go ahead for any reason, what's in their terms and conditions, and at what stage of cancellation do you have to pay in full?

Wow, that's some list – so would you rather do it yourself and not bother with an event organiser? Well, all the questions I've listed above are what you need to ask of your suppliers, e.g. your musicians, magicians, entertainers, caterers etc. if you are doing the organising yourself. So do you want the bother, do you have the time, or would you rather hand it over to someone who can co- ordinate it all for you, saving you time and hassle, and letting you be a guest at your own event? Both options are attractive at some points in your life, and it also will depend on whether you are able to cede some control!

9 FABULOUS FUNCTIONS – GOING TO THE BALL AND HAVING A BALL!

So, armed with the knowledge I've set out above, do you feel confident in organising a fabulous function? I really hope so! Of course, there are thousands of books written on the subject of event planning, and this book is not for someone who wants to delve deeply into the myriad of events, both social and corporate that are organised, planned and managed throughout the world.

Rather, it is a simple canter through the types of events we are likely to want to or have to organise during our lifetime. I hope that it is helpful and gives you the tools to organise a fabulous party, wedding or work do.

If you would like to know more about me and my company DezEvents.com and how I can help you plan your next event, please contact me at Deborah@dezevents.com or call 07990 751857 or visit my website at www.dezevents.com

ABOUT THE AUTHOR

Deborah Granville, founder and director of DezEvents.com, has been a singer, lawyer, charity professional and now event planner and blogger. She has run all kinds of events, from a large scale tour of a medical research facility attended by the then Prime Minister Tony Blair, motivational weekend workshops, charity balls with celebrities and politicians, quizzes, film showings and networking events, as well as receptions at the House of Lords. Deborah relishes a challenge both in her professional as well as her personal life, and has taken part in a 60K walk around London as well as a 10K run and an abseil. She lives in London with her family.

Thank you's

Firstly, I'd like to thank relationship counsellor Shelley Whitehead, my fellow Women in Business member, who very kindly and generously gave me a copy of *Become a Key Person of Influence* by Daniel Priestley, which spurred me on to write this book.

Secondly, many thanks to writer and author Marilyn Messik, my fellow Athena member, who suggested the title of this book and provided me with much encouragement and support.

Thirdly, thank you to Laura Dowers of Blue Laurel for her sterling work, encouragement and patience.

And finally, to my family and friends who have had to put up with my ramblings over the last few months, but who have held me accountable for this book, even if they didn't know it!

And if you loved this book , or even just liked it, please consider "liking" it on Amazon and even reviewing it – I would be eternally grateful!

- Deborah Granville, November 2015

DEBORAH GRANVILLE

Printed in Great Britain
by Amazon.co.uk, Ltd.,
Marston Gate.